The Story of
Ruby Lee

This is the story of Ruby Lee.

She was a very smart little girl indeed.

She liked to play her video games. Which she held

in her hand both night and day.

There was not much else that she liked to do

if you asked she would say "I dont want to."

The Story of
Ruby Lee

This is the story of Ruby Lee.

She was a very smart little girl indeed.

She liked to play her video games. Which she held

in her hand both night and day.

There was not much else that she liked to do

if you asked she would say "I dont want to."

BLEEP
BLOOP
BLEEP

She would go to school and the teacher would say,

"Ruby Lee, could you please put your game away?"

And in a quite bored and bothered way,

"I don't want to so I'm not going to," she would say.

September
Sun Mon Tue Wed Thu Fri Sat
1 2 3 4 5 6
7 8 9 10 11 12 13
14 15 16 17 18 19 20
21 22 23 24 25 26 27
28 29 30
20
× 10
TAP TAP
bleep
BLOOP
BLEEP

At recess time when all the children were playing,

Ruby Lee would sit in the corner gaming.

They would ask her, "Ruby Lee, don't you want to go climbing

or pretend that we're airplanes swooping and flying?"

"Oh no," as she stared at the video screen, "my adventures in this game

are all that i need!"

BLOOP
BLEEP
BLOP

at dinner, at breakfast all she saw was that screen.

Even at bed time when she was supposed to be sleeping,

Ruby Lee would be under her covers BLEEPING.

Many springs bloomed...and playful winters passed...

New games were consumed

and HIGH scores surpassed.

HIGH SCORE!!

And as the years went by,
Ruby Lee had grown up.
She lived all alone
in a sad little slump.

Her skin looked quite grey, her eyes shriveled up
from squinting at the screen that she loved so much.
No children, no sunshine.
No laughing, no crying.
Just bleeps and bloops from her games
she was playing.

bleep
BLOOP
BLEEP

And when it was time to pay last respects

no one was there as you would expect.

The only connection that she ever made

was plugging in her game at the end of the day.

So remember this story and take great heed

or you could end up like poor Ruby Lee...

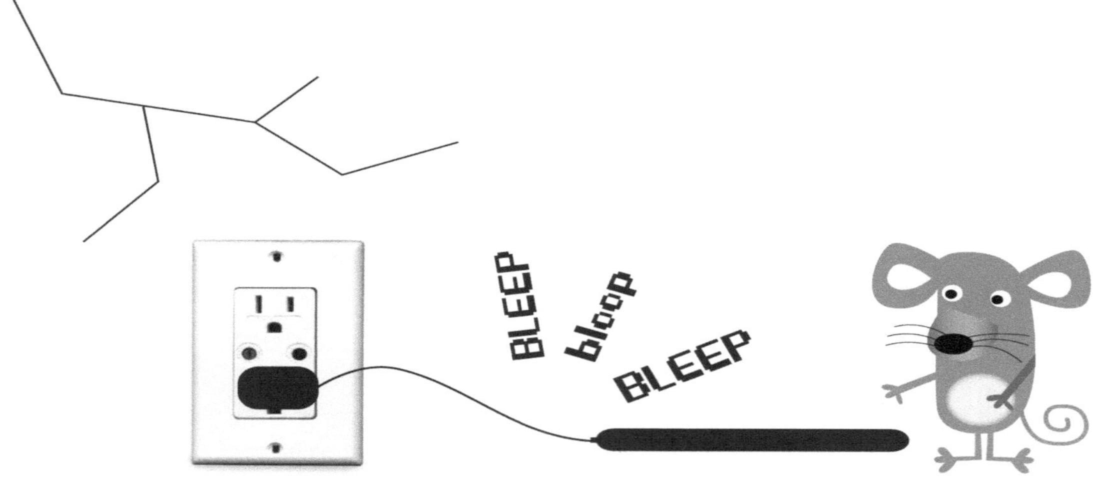

GAME OVER